Upon Entering
the *Kingdom*

Evangelist Nicole Mangum

DEDICATION

This book is dedicated to my God. The opener of my heart. The writer of my destiny. The love in my life.

Table of Contents

Evangelist Nicole Mangum

Prologue

There is a place in God where you can see miracles every day. It is a place of grace and spirit. It is only accessible to those who have been born again. Born again is a an actual state. It is not as simple as laying aside habits. It is more than a change in thought, though it does begin with a thought. Thoughts of meeting our Lord and Savior Jesus.

The thinking is what propels you. The thinking on a love that seems so far away, until he feels your longing and adoration for him and turns his face to you. Once he has his face to you he starts moving. The closer he gets the more conflict comes into your life. It is as if all the forces of darkness have set themselves against you making the connection with the one your heart adores.

As he moves your heart burns as it feels his momentum. Your soul knows he's here. Your soul knows. My soul cried out, "Daddy" before I even saw his face. It's a wonder I ponder on often, My soul knows more about my connection with the LORD than my natural person.

My soul knows how to prepare for my visitations. My soul knows when I need to get quite and wait on the LORD. My soul is spirit. I use this spirit to try the spirit by the spirit. My soul is perfectly in tuned to my Savior and God.

Rebirth

Upon Entering the Kingdom

Luke 12:32 "Fear not little flock, for it is your father's good pleasure to give you the kingdom."

My Soul blossomed from an empty shell
Piece by piece the struggles
and burdens of this world
Fell away...like the dropping of a robe
I entered into the Kingdom...
And the souls of old folk, Saints, and Angels
Came to share in my happiness
They rejoiced with me
I felt so welcomed as they said
"Hello Darling, we're so glad you make it."
What a wonderful place God's heaven.
Yes, what a wonderful glorious place

He Brought Heaven Down to Me

John 14:23 " Jesus answered and said unto him, If a man love me, he will keep my words: and my Father will love him, and we will come unto him, and make our abode with him."

He brought heaven down to me
I wasn't sleeping.
I was wide awake.
Before I saw his face,
My soul cried, "Daddy!"
It was so amazing,
My heart was full and blazing
Touched by my love
He brought heaven from above

Heavenly Accessibility

Luke 17:21 "Neither shall they say, Lo here! Or, lo there! For behold, the Kingdom of God is within you."

My soul resides in heaven. I breathe heaven's air. My Father is always accessible to me. He always hears me. I have endured the test of faith. I chose him every time. His heart is towards me always.

A New Creature

John 3:7 "Marvel not that I said unto thee, Ye must be born again."

It is through much suffering
That you become a new creature in Christ
It is as if every part within you shall fail
And through much pain
You learn to praise the creator more abundantly
After losing your natural mind
You are given the true mind of Christ
And once your body is so ragged and torn
The LORD will wrap you in swaddling clothes
To bandage your wounds
And one day you will awaken
Shedding the sinful body
As if emerging from a cocoon
And like a butterfly you will have wings
And on this earth you shall see and feel
The Kingdom of Heaven

The Spirit

John 3:5 "Except a man be born of water and of spirit he cannot enter into the Kingdom of God."

The Spirit of the LORD is all around me
I cannot keep still
The Spirit of the LORD is deep inside me
My whole soul is filled
Sometimes I want to shout
Sometimes I want to cry
Sometimes I want to run
I feel like I can fly
How could I turn away
From all the love you gave me
How could I return
to the life from which you saved me
My feet are planted firm
I shall not be moved
I will serve you LORD
Until heaven and earth are moved

Glory

Isaiah 60:1 "ARISE shine for thy light is come, and the glory of the LORD is risen upon thee."

I am like the wind, so soft, so light,
My life has become an endless dream
In the midst of trouble I am safe
Weapons melt before me like a spring rain
I am peace, I am peace personified
I lounge in the eye of the storm
I am love, love overflowing unto the ground
Washing away hate with a quiet storm
Can you hear the peace
Can you hear the love
It is God
God with us

His Grace is Sufficient

John 8:7 "...the words that I speak unto you they are spirit and they are life

From this broken down body
life shoots forth like a tree
A tree planted by the river of Jordan
We are seeds
Seeds planted in the dirt and soil
Of this corrupt world
And it is the constant showering of rain
And the beating down of the Son
That allows us to live again
Not as before
But as new creatures
Spirit men and women
Connected directly to the love of God
By the union of his Holy Spirit to our souls
Be free, for the Son has given it to you
Your freedom in a bound world
New Life, New Creature, True Creature
Full of Light

I live

John 5:25 "...and the dead shall hear the voice of the Son of God and they that hear shall live."

I awoke
Praising God in the most beautiful way
My movements full of grace
My voice like an angel
I swayed like the wind
Bowed like the limbs of a willow
The coolness of the Lord surrounded me
We were one like leaves floating on the wind
What Peace
What Love
Love manifest as the wind
covered me with peace and filled my soul
I am transformed a new creature
Holy and acceptable
I walk in spirit and truth
I am light, a watchtower that cannot be hid
Only shine beautifully
Flow beautifully
Love beautifully

I shall give me

2 Corinthians 6:16 "...for ye are the temple of the living God...I will dwell in them, and walk in them."

This beauty that you see
Is far deeper than it appears
For it has been shaped
by the washing away of sin
And as the river flows through the Grand Canyon
My Father has created yet another master piece
That is me
Worthy to house the finer things
The Water of Life, the Holy Spirit of God
I know I shine bright like the Son
It is the righteousness of the Saints
That are shining down on me
What else could I build for the LORD?
When he fills the whole world
What royal tapestry of silk or wool
Could I use for his feet
When all he desired was me

My Cup Overfloweth

Psalms 34:8 "O Taste and see that the LORD is good."

I have tasted and seen
That the LORD is good
So I asked for a cup
I drank and drank
Until it seemed like something in me burst
It started at the pit of my soul
Flowing upward past my heart
It flowed up through my out stretched
Hands giving praise to God
It flowed from my mouth
My ears and my tongue
Everlasting life I know I've won
The living waters flow through me
And I am planted like a tree
By the river of Jordan

Planted

Psalm 22:30 "A seed shall serve him; it shall be accounted to the Lord for a generation."

A seed
Such a small commonly thing
But once planted, watered, and fed
By the Son
Produces such a magnificent and wonderful thing
Something uncorrupt and straightened
Smooth no longer ragged
Peace no more chaos
Love no more hate
Quiet within the storm

Grace

Ephesians 2:8 "for by grace are ye saved through faith, not of yourselves, it is the gift of God."

No greater love than
Jesus laying down his life for my soul
I cannot comprehend the hardship that it tolled
He has always loved me
Forgiving again, again, and again,
My disobedience and defiance
My swerving right and left
Not once did he deny my entry back onto his path
Not once did he turn me away
My repentance not accept
Oh Jesus thank you for your mercy,
your Grace and your love
Because without either my victory
I would not have won

Take Hold of me

Psalms 31:18 "For I will declare mine iniquity, I will be sorry
for my sin."

Lord what are you saying to me
I'm lost in this storm
It's dark and I can't see
I'm so full of sin I can't hear you
I'm so wrapped up in myself I can't feel you
I've got this cloud on my soul
I'm cold
I'm not strong
I need your arms
Take hold of me

The Master's Rest

Matthews 11:28 "Come unto me all ye that labor and are
heavy laden, and I will give you rest."

There is no love
More beautiful than yours
There is no power more lovely to behold
Within your arms I've found protection
Within your arms I'm safe from harm
Journey with me
Into my Master's Peace
Let us stand in his presence
And from life have relief

All This For Me

Psalms 37:4 "Delight thyself also in the LORD and he shall give thee the desires of your heart."

What is this glory
That has been showered down on me
It is the love of God
The Father's love
I am his child
He carries me in his bosom
I am safe
For the first time in my life
I have no fear
Every need is met before I speak
I shall never leave this place

Evangelist Nicole Mangum

Before Grace

Nicole's Liberation

1 Corinthians 7:21 "Are you a slave? Don't let that worry you–but if you get a chance to be free, take it.

All I ever wanted was to be free
Take some time out and get to know me
Search my soul to my own self be true
Try to heal all the pain I've been through
I know this heart of mine with love it overflows
Who I connects with only God knows
It seems though only the wrong respond
Or maybe wrong is of what I've grown fond
What I do know is this cycle has to end
And today I will begin Nicole's liberation

Limbo

1 Samuel 1:15 "And Hannah answered and said, No, my lord, I *am* a woman of a sorrowful spirit: I have drunk neither wine nor strong drink, but have poured out my soul before the LORD."

I don't want to think
for then I will feel and if I feel
it must be real
I don't want reality right now
let me stay endlessly in
this state of limboed
nothingness
until I am able to deal
with this thing called life
a captured day dream
were in my mind everything
is the way it should be
I am master of my domain
ruler of my realm
queen of my court
beautiful free?
To no degree
oh no a thought
my day dream is lost

When Roses Grew No Thorns

Esther 1:12 "But the queen Vashti refused to come at the king's commandment by *his* chamberlains: therefore was the king very wroth, and his anger burned in him."

There is a twisted fairytale sprang from the start of time
Where roses grew smooth stems no burrows could you find
She still grew silken petals with perfume scented smell
Her life was one of royalty no marks of fate dispelled
Until...Man began to covet rose...to keep her as his own...
He sought to cut her down placing her in crystal bowls
He sought to trap her essence by syphoning her soul
And rose began transforming staying beautiful
While growing hard and cold
From this a phrase was coined about a woman scorned
And it was taken from the fairy-tale
"When Roses grew no thorns"

Love

Love

Genesis 2:18 "God said it is not good for the man to be alone."

Whoever said love does not hurt
Has never been in love
To live my life without you near
Takes strength from God above
My heart longs for your kisses
My body longs for your touch
What God has put together
Should never be apart
Our first father Adam
Was not tricked or deceived
He just could not imagine
His life without Eve

Anxious

Song of Solomon 5:2 "I sleep but my heart waketh..."

Your love
Takes me to heights of escatasy
I am afloat
On a river that runs into paradise
I am a leaf
Caught up in an autumn breeze
Flowing upward then
Slowly
Slowly
Slowly
Falling back down to earth
Anxiously awaiting its next ascension

I love you

Song of Solomon 7:10 " I am my beloveds and his desire is toward me."

I love you
Like the earth loves the rain
You love is cool, Refreshing
Thirst quenching
And
Just like Earth
I could not survive
If you love stopped falling
I would just dry up and die
Becoming a barren desert

Soft

Song of Solomon 2:6 " His left hand is under my head and his right hand doth embrace me."

Your love is soft
Like a cool breeze on a warm day
Like the sound of a quiet storm at midnight
Through a cracked windowsill
Like water,
Flowing over a parched tongue
Like a mother's breast
To her lover and her young

My Lord

Ephesians 5:33 "...and the wife see that she reverence her husband."

My Lord leads me
My husband my head
I follow closely behind him
He gladly allows me to walk beside him
But I choose the safety of behind him
Where I am free to watch his strength
As he forges ahead
Clearing our path
So I can walk without stumbling
I am his Queen
He is my King
He falls that I may stand

With You I am King

Ephesians 5:28 "He that loveth his wife loveth himself."

When I look at you
I see a part of me that is perfect
Strong yet gentle
Though I have the fate of man
I elevate you as a queen
This world beats me down so profusely
It takes everything within me
You replenish me
Without you I am just a man
With you I am a King
Worthy of the finest things
Your love makes me walk with pride
Stare evil right within the eye
Because within you my prize lies
My seed barer, my lover, my wife

This Love

Ephesians 5:23 "...for the husband is the head of the wife..."

What kind of love is this
The more I give
The more is taken
What kind of love is this
When it feels like my heart is aching
To stand against the wind
To speak unto the storm
To overcome the world
For the sake of a little girl
Who at the start of time
Was deceived by a lie
That was planted in her mind
But this love reversed time
So that everything you see
Would result in good for you and me
And death was overcome
Before it was begun

She

Genesis 24:67 "...and she became his wife; and he loved her

When she smiles my world is brighter
When she is strong my strength is mightier
When she breathes I breathe lighter
I was lost and she became my guider
Is this what HE meant
When from heaven He sent
Me this help meet
Whose lips are the richest sweet
I have ever tasted
Whose love is the strongest
I have ever faced
It humbles me to my knees
Do all I can to please she
That this grace may never leave me
For I was thirst and she gave me
Straight from the hand of God our Father
A taste of the living waters

This is the Day

Psalms 118:24 "This is the day which the LORD hath made;
We will rejoice and be glad in it."

This is the day that's so full of grace
There is joy in this day, Peace in this day
On this day
When two lonely hearts
Have finally become a part of one
A life has just begun
This is the day
With the passage of time
And the opening of my eyes
I began to see
That you were a part of me
Part of my destiny
I never would have dreamed
That you were the king
Waiting to carry me into my destiny
Do many times you'd smile and pass by
Well you were just planting seeds
No the Father's love has rained on me
Your love has become our tree
Rooted deep inside of HE
I am so ready to be your queen
You are my destiny

Happy Anniversary

Ephesians 5:22 "Husbands love your wives..."

A woman was made from love to be loved
It is the only way she will flourish and grow
When you look at me you see a man who loves you
A man that hurts when you hurt
And laughs when you laugh
I need you. I love you
I am your Adam
You are the rib that was taken from me so long ago
Now you are returned
I was bruised and worn,
but with you I am restored
You are my Eve the mother of all living
Everything I place in your hand multiplies
You make my burden easier
With you I will till the ground
As you wipe the sweat from my brow
We will create our piece of
The Kingdom of God

Wonderful

Isaiah 9:6 "...and his name shall be called Wonderful..."

I held wonderful by the palm of its hand
It was tall handsome
With a smile like a three year old at Christmas
It felt good to the touch
Made you feel safe
And kept you warm
Wonderful made you want to take each day
Like you were loving for the first time
It was so good, you wanted it to last forever
And just when you thought it would fade
Wonderful makes things wonderful all over again

A Word From the LORD

Vanity

Psalm 94:11"The Lord knoweth the thoughts of man, That they are vanity."

With all your titles and degrees
If you have not love you have nothing
I cannot understand
When God places within your hand
A child that is so innocent,
a blessing that is heaven sent
yet with arrogance you disregard
and write them off as county wards
Yet Sunday's you shout, "I believe"
And with all your titles and degrees
You have not love so you have nothing
The titles you greatly aspire
and the praise and glory you desire
Mean nothing when your soul retires
Your body is laid down to rest
And before the Father you must attest
It shall all be in vain as our Father's voice proclaims
"I never knew you;
You see, My righteousness you did not seek
My children you have left for dead
But by my grace they still got fed
Get away from me unrighteous seed
You worker of iniquity
And from Hell you lift up your eyes
And no title there will compromise
Your position there within the fire

Great Teacher

Job 27:11 "I will teach you by the hand of God..."

Thank God for a Great Teacher
You have a story to tell
That through great struggle and pain
Righteousness did prevail
One night when you retired
A Miracle transpired
In your heart you understood
That there is no greater good
Than to give of yourself
And hope later one would accept
This wonderful gift you chose to give
So a better life they may live
Just like Christ on Christmas Day
Was born to show the way
And an anointing each year is born
On each glorious Christmas morn
And I wish it well for you and
The ones you love great and few

We are One Body

Philippians 2:2 "that ye be liked minded, having the same love being of one accord one mind..."

Come inside my family as you are
We are all the same Children of God
O I see the deception the devil
would have me believe
But, God has given me my sight
It is you I see before me
Your soul is just like mine longing to be free
We are strangers here this is not our eternity
Please come inside my family
There is plenty of space
The father has given us a double portion
Of his mercy and grace
We are the righteousness of God
Redeemed of the human race

Rejoice

Psalm 23:2 "...he maketh me to lie down in green pastures..."

The harvest is in. It is time to live
The meadows are green. I shall run through them
With my arms raised in praise to the Lord
My soul has longed for this day
The Savior has returned, and with him his reward
Wo cares about the tears shed through the years
They are being wiped away never to return
In the form of despair
Tears of joy will never cease to be
My father it was you, You were here all the time
Leading me, Ordering me, rearranging me
Storm after storm, hurt after hurt, loss after loss,
To stand in your glory, by your glory
Because of your Grace

My Children

2 Corinthians 6:18 "Ye shall be my sons and daughters, saith the Lord Almighty."

Do you think I will leave you alone
In this would without my love
I love you
Do you think I have forsaken you
I made you
Do you think your cries fall upon deaf ears
I hear you
I fill the whole entire world, and
My love is from everlasting to everlasting
I have withheld nothing for the sake of your souls
Before you were ... I love you
Unto death ... I love you
When you return to me ... I love you

Life's Question

Job 7:1 "...is there not an appointed time to man upon the earth?"

If heaven is the ultimate goal
Of a servant of God
Why is losing someone you love
So painful and hard
Could it be that we in our selfishness
Want to keep them here
Never to reach their mansion
With streets paved of gold
To sip milk from honeycombs
It's hard not to see their face
It's hard to know they won't be home
But if you're quiet and at peace
You can still feel their souls

Thy Salvation Cometh

Exodus 16:12 "I have heard the murmurings of the children of Israel."

I looked upon you and cried,
"Why are my children suffering?
Is there no balm in Gilead?
Is Israel a servant?
Is he a home born slave?
Then I saw that no one lead you to the balm
Nor bothered to fetch it for you
I saw how you were distressed
Sheep without a shepherd
Unwashed in need of salt
Behold your salvation cometh
With him is your reward
You shall be cleansed your beauty restored

Going Through

Genesis 42:36 "...All these things are against me."

Momma can you hear me
Can you feel me in your soul
I'm trying hard to keep my head up
I'm trying hard not to let go
I know the bed you make
In it you must lay down
But all this pain and loss
Has got me level to the ground
Just don't stop praying me through
I know God spared me because of you
I will lift up my head up to the hills
Try hard with faith to discipline my will
And to your love I will hang on
Until my Savior sends me home

Freedman

2 Corinthians 3:14 "But their minds were blinded..."

January 1, 1863 I am a product of Slavery
And though I have been freed, freedom eludes me
You are my master. I am your slave
This I know. Freedom ... I do not understand.
Three hundred years went into making me
And the stripes on my back bare witness of my initiation
Into this order of the slave
This order of the freedman...I do not understand.
It is now January 1, 2006
And I am still the product of slavery
I have been freed one hundred and forty three years
And Freedom still eludes me
You are still my master. I am still your slave.
Though I live in a freedman's house
Receive a freedman's wage
The drugs in my veins and the darkness of my soul
Defines me as a bound man
I envied you and your freedom
The harvest that you yield
I longed to eat the fruit of my labor
But my limbs failed to produce and the danger
of being cut down remained constantly before me
Then one day I walked into the Son
and the brightness of his glory
exposed your evil crime
so wicked and so vile
In leaving the shackles on the freedman's mind

A Little Straight

Colossians 2:8 "Beware lsest any man spoil you through Philosophy and vain deceit after the tradition of men..."

In the world of crookedness
Crooked love, crooked teachers
Crooked faith, crooked preachers
I'm trying to give the world a little straight
Straight talk, straight truth, straight faced
We're losing our children to a world
That is cruel hard and blurred
To rectify we must start with truth
No more Santa Clause
No more fairies for their tooth
Today is the day to change their fate
If we start with a little straight

Farewell Young Soldiers

1 Kings 20:25 "You must also raise an army like the one you lost–horse for horse and chariot for chariot–so we can fight Israel on the plains."

Farewell young soldiers
Strong courageous and refined
May your journey be swift
and your return undefiled
May our hearts stay strong
as we send you on your way
and we hold back our tears
Avoiding emotional displays
May God watch over your souls
And keep your spirits bright
May he send guardian angels
to steer your weapons right
May our leader realize that
in his method is madness
May his conspiracy be exposed
His orders ceased and desist
May a sudden act of fate
plunder all of this turmoil
and our young soldiers guiltlessly
returned to their home soil

Love in a Name

Christ Jesus

John 14:2 "...I go to prepare a place for you."

Come go with me
High above the trees, where
rivers flow eternally
Inside a space
So filled with grace
Thanksgiving and God's mercy
Just visualize first in your mind
Each blessing being answered
Soon you will see
Unveiled to thee
Something glorious and miraculous

Nicole

Luke 1:45 "...blessed is she that believed..."

Now I wanted the LORD
I wanted no other thing
Confused and alone, until
Omnipotence came
Love laid me to rest
Elevated my mind
Now I am awaken
The old me
Frozen in time
For I move throughout eternity
Peeking here and there
Reborn a new creature
To live forever and ever

Clarice

1 Corinthians 13:13 "and the greatest of these is love."

Close your eyes and visualize
Laying down with me
Above the sky, where
Rivers flow crystal clear, from
Inside an angel's wings we peer, while
Coming into the promised land
Entrance is granted and
We can see where we will spend eternity
And now Clarice, I hope you see
My love is for always, but
When always will cease to be
My love will never fade

Debbie

Matthew 14:14 "If ye shall ask anything in my name
I will do it.?

Did you make your request known ...in
Entirety to our LORD
Before his throne of grace
Brought from deep within your heart
It is no mystery to him
Each wish he already sees
But you must first speak them
To show that you believe

Demetria

Ephesians 5:28 "So ought men to love their wives as their own bodies."

Day after day
Each morning of my life
My heart beats strong for you
Each day I promise
To provide, because my love is true
Remember in the Garden of Eden
If I were
Adam and you were Eve
I never would have failed
To defend your honor night and day
And light would have prevailed

Gwen

Isaiah 62:11 "...Behold thy salvation cometh..."

God is with you
When it's hard to believe
Even at your
Notorious times
His eyes have always seen
Your sacrifice your test
They have not been in vain
For you shall reap a harvest
Of his blessed Latter Rain

Lakyra T. Garth

Hebrews 13:2 "Be not forgetful to entertain strangers for thereby some have entertained angels unawares."

Suffer the
Little children to come unto me
Angels I bring forth through thee
Kept hidden from the eyes of man
Your divine identity and plan, shall be
Revealed in God's on time
Awaken O daughter of Zion
Take thy place and lead the way
God has created
A new thing
Revelations shall come by woman
The children lead the way
Heaven's gates are open
By God's love, mercy, and grace

Mary

Proverbs 11:16 "A gracious woman retaineth honor..."

My heart can feel your pain
Although my eyes can't see...and
Right before you spoke the words
Your Savior turned his face to thee
He saw his beautiful daughter
Stand up against the world
And he was very proud of
His precious baby girl
No prayer has gone unanswered
No wish has he declined
And now you will receive it all
Right before your eyes

Lady Doris

Proverbs 14:1 "Every wise woman buildeth her house..."

Lady wisdom you have a foundation
And not it is time to build
Do not delay any longer
Your harvest is ready to yield
Deposit your love with interest
Open up your heart
Receive the latter rain of blessing
Increase that will never part
Shine for your salvation has come

Mary

Proverbs 31:26 "She openeth her mouth with wisdom; and in her tongue is the law of kindness."

Mary, did you know
Angels are at your side...on your
Right and on your left
Your protection God provides
My mind never wondered
Why you walked in such glory
You spoke with such strong love
I knew that it was sent from
Heaven up above

Ora Lee

1 Corinthians 15:51 "Behold I show you a mystery; we shall not all sleep, but we shall all be changed."

One day love will lift you
Right before our eyes
Away into God's heaven
Letting this world's pain subside
Eternal life with the Master
Earth is not your home
And deep within our hearts
Your presence we will long
But in the midnight hour
You'll visit in our dreams
And it can be so real if only we believe

Serita P. Lane

Psalm 27:13 "I had fainted unless I believed to see the goodness of the Lord in the Land of the living."

Shout Hallelujah
Every day of your life, your
Reward is at hand
Into the Master's Rest you've
Taken comfort
Adhering to his every command
Peace unto you my sister
Let God's praises ring loud
And new beginning and
New life
Eternal he has allowed

Shirley

Isaiah 62:12 "And they shall call them, the holy people, the redeemed of the lord..."

Such a long journey
How much you've overcame
Instead of death you chose life
Relinquishing past pains
Live,...for
Each day is new
Your yesterdays are just that
No one can longer hurt you
You are far past that
For you have overcame
The whole entire world...and
You're forever in God's rest
His precious little girl

Vera

Jeremiah 31:22 "for the Lord hath created a new thing in the earth, a woman shall compass a man."

O what a glorious
Victory you have won...in each and
Every test you've glorified the Son
Restoration is here...just
Around the bend
New life, new beginning
To which there is no end
Fear not God's little soldier
He's right by your side
And There is where he'll always be
For the rest of your life

Sister Shelton

Jeremiah 20:9 "...his word was in my heart as a burning fire shut up on my bones."

Shine forth your light
It is not intended to be hidden
So many all-around you are in
Total darkness
Experience you have
Right from the hand of God
So why deny the sheep the food
Home grown form deep inside of you
Election you obtained over a year ago
Lord Jesus anointed you
To teach the truth in whole
Only you can bring forth this message
No one else has lived your life
So deliver it with power
God's ambassador of light

Sister Banks

Isaiah 62:10 "...lift up a standard for the people..."

Silently you waited while
Intently looking in
Slow to speak quick to listen
Teaching the flock as your soul glistens
Express your gratitude, yet
Relay to the congregation the truth
Brought to you from
Above by God's angels
No more turning a deaf ear pretending not to see
Keep your hand in God's for through you he
Shall speak
To give them all a warning
That they must change their ways
The Savior has returned it is the final days

Shumeka and Eric

Mark 10:9 "What therefor God hath joined together let no man put asunder."

So I shall share my life with you
Holding on to these words of truth
Unconditional is our love
My soul rejoiced the day
Eternally you vowed to stay
Keeping me forever yours
Angels will clear our path
As we journey hand and hand
No weapon formed will dare trespass
Didn't God give you to me....for
Ever after and eternity
Right here we both shall be
Inside the Master's hand
Complete from beginning to end

Carina, Carina

Isaiah 9:6 ' For unto us a child is born."

Can't wait to see this child
Adorned with rings of gold
Remember children are from God
Into your womb now bestowed
Now do not doubt your blessing
Always have faith and believe
Carina God has a gift for you
Arriving from you childhood dreams
Rico is included
I know you love him so
Now let his love take over
And the blessings overflow

Clarence

Matthew 5:36 "..Be not afraid only believe."

Clap your hands and stomp your feet
Lift your hands up with praise
Arriving from our Master
Rewards Deliverance and Grace
Ending all hurt misery and pain
No weapon formed has prospered
Can you feel the Latter Rain?
Each drop you should saver
Each day will be brand new
And you shall receive it all from God
A life that is brand new

Rhonda

Mark 10:16 "and he took them up in his arms, Put his hands upon them, and blessed them."

Righteousness is measured by your faith
Hope your faith is overflowing
One need not ask another
No one else bares your anointing
Don't doubt what he has for you
A wish a dream comes true
A life that is a brand new
Is waiting just for you
Straight from the Master's hand

Carolyn and Keith

Song of Solomon 8:6 "...for Love is a strong as death."

Can the wind blow
And the earth not know
Remember this when
One of you is alone
Love my dears once planted
Yearly yields
No famine or drought only wide open fields
And love my darlings
Needs spirit to survive
Don't you know love is divine
Keep trying to separate you'll only draw close
Each pull only strengthens the knot in the rope
It's divinely tied
Together by three
Hope, Love, Faith, the Holy Trinity

Kelsie

Esther 2:17 "He set the royal crown upon your head and made her queen..."

Keep your eyes on the prize
Each and everyday
Life has dealt you a blow
So God shall show you the way
I know it seems so far away, but
Eventually you shall see
That God has blessed and exalted you
My child you are a queen

Evangelist Nicole Mangum

www.ingramcontent.com/pod-product-compliance
Lightning Source LLC
Chambersburg PA
CBHW021139020426
42331CB00005B/828